# THE SIGN OF THE RAM
## O-JEREMIAH AGBAAKIN

This is a work of fiction. All names, characters, places, and incidents are a product of the author's imagination. Any resemblance to real events or persons, living or dead, is entirely coincidental.

Published by Akashic Books
©2023 O-Jeremiah Agbaakin
ISBN: 978-1-63614-126-8

All rights reserved
Printed in China
First printing

Akashic Books
Brooklyn, New York
Instagram, Twitter, Facebook: @AkashicBooks
E-mail: info@akashicbooks.com
Website: www.akashicbooks.com

African Poetry Book Fund
*Prairie Schooner*
University of Nebraska
110 Andrews Hall
Lincoln, Nebraska 68588

## TABLE OF CONTENTS

*Preface by 'Gbenga Adeoba* 5

isaac's confession  9
deus ex machina  10
rebirth  11
miliaria  12
father's apology  13
light-years  14
ode to the serpent  16
post-fluvial myth with the veil  18
mirror  19
good friday  21
devotion  22
epistolary  23
necromancy  25

*Acknowledgments* 26

## PREFACE
*by 'Gbenga Adeoba*

In Nigerian poet O-Jeremiah Agbaakin's *The Sign of the Ram*, we begin with a confession that is bifurcated in its logic. A portion of the opening verse, the head or tail notion that it suggests, is telling in this regard: "at the toss of a coin, i would do anything / to save myself." ("Isaac's confession"). The confession is one that foreshadows the slant of Agbaakin's poetic exploration in this chapbook: an interrogation of physical and emotional violence in religion; a quest to understand and articulate trauma across shifting geographies—fatherhood and a father-son relationship being both triggers and anchors for this inquiry:

> you must know that i wouldn't turn a hungry knife in the flesh.
> you must know that i had no say in all this. you must
> know that i heard a wolf call & i couldn't resist for
> it sounded so holy.
>
> ("father's apology")

The other side of the prefatory confession is anchored by a pursuit of meaning, a sense of self, and new beginnings. It is through this perspective that we see the speaker's keen awareness of his quest's complexity and human fallibility. In the inaugurating poem, the speaker tells us how he betrayed a friend and orients us to his consciousness of his flaw(s):

> i confess, i've confessed a friend to the edge
>     of a teacher's rage, *okoko,* the school's pilate,
> armed with his quiver of canes.
>
> ("isaac's confession")

It seems to me, then, that even as he is eloquent in his interrogation of violence and trauma, Agbaakin's speaker privileges accountability over condemnation. It is evinced by one of his titles, "father's apology," and the father-speaker in that poem. He keeps an eye firmly on compassion, reclamation, and restoration through imagination and creative gestures. In this sense, his speaker unearths memories with ardor and marked deftness. In multiple poems, Agbaakin attends to the dailiness and rituals of childhood. Familial memories are thus significant entry points for the speaker's investigation of trauma and pain, and a quest for meaning and healing:

> but years after that night, the mice took
> the house, sniping uncle's chained tiger
> generator wires with their incisors

("ode to the serpent")

Nonetheless, it is also in this attention to family members that a possible verdict regarding the speaker's self-engrossment is subverted and rendered unconvincing. Sufficient human interest is offered, and the reader is made to care:

> years later, we left.
> she, too, left us. years later, the machine
> coughed again with my auntie's final
> breath of soot and poisoned lungs.

("ode to the serpent")

Agbaakin's speaker sees and knows things and is given to empathy. He cares about both humans and nonhumans in the household. His posture acknowledges and insists on a multiverse; alongside the familial milieu, the dynamics of relationships and family, nonhumans figure considerably in his curated worlds and assemblage—fairies, stars, ghouls, fish, and snakes; a Yoruba god; the "euthanized granny's last goat." ("deus ex machina")

Agbaakin's poems demonstrate a poetics of possibilities. This creative outlook appears in his language and attention to oral traditions and Yoruba myth:

> i crouch under the safe dome of the sky. *ọba
> k'òso, ọba k'òso.* a god hangs from a missing
> rope.

("devotion")

The verbal dexterity with which Yoruba and English syntax and rhythm become twinned in the poems recalls what literary theorist Jahan Ramazani has described as the hybridization of muses. Remarkably, then, Agbaakin is attuned at the core to the life of words and stretches their limits; he puts both languages in conversation and asks us to heed the ensuing music. These sonic and linguistic dimensions significantly underscore the skillfulness and creative poise that mark the work in this chapbook. But equally striking is the sheer range of allusions and influences that undergird his work. "good friday" recasts a famous line by William Wordsworth, and in "devotion," he borrows and is in conversation with a verse from a peer's poem. Biblical imageries and references also loom large in these poems; yet, his speaker reminds us of doubt at every turn, offering faith and religious imageries as only one node in his worldview and creative framework. We find, for example, a painterly impulse in his contemplative exploration, as art references further animate one of the biblical stories—the sacrifice of Isaac.

The distance that appears to mark Agbaakin's inquiry in this chapbook is tempered by what the body carries beyond. Although in pursuit of a fresh start, his speaker is compelled by remaining scars of childhood "heat rash" to return to memory. Embodied markers of a troubling past are thus at the fore at a tattoo shop where the speaker finds a transformative transaction to be dicey:

> you'll beg the snake to teach
> you how to shed the miliaria
> but it'll speak of the pain of losing
> everything, the brief shame of nakedness
> as you wait for new skin
>
> ("miliaria")

In this quest for new beginnings, Agbaakin offers a brilliant and riveting body of work from what the speaker in "isaac's confession" describes as "what's left of the fire." His writing is imbued with a steady vision and is a testament to his remarkable talent and greater works to come.

## ISAAC'S CONFESSION

at the toss of a coin, i would do anything
      to save myself. father, don't we burn enough

offering to keep you warm? the ash survives
      what's left of the fire. the smoke puffs in vain.

i confess, i've confessed a friend to the edge
      of a teacher's rage, *okoko*, the school's pilate,

armed with his quiver of canes. i confessed
      after breaking my bread for him yearlong, or

was it after the deed? i cannot remember what
      came before but i was tender once. it's so easy

that he was already stricken with fever before
      assembly. what'd god do with a missing sacrifice?

the god of raised whip, armed with his quiver
      of canes. what can you do with me, a beast with

no heart, long dead even before the knife. a fire
      won't torch a thing like that. i confess: i have too

much heart left in me. believe me, i am marked
      with the sign of the ram. you must not forsake me.

## DEUS EX MACHINA

an angel lets down
a rope with a neat noose
at the edge. a hole could
also mean escape like
the kind incision when we
euthanized granny's last goat.
not the hole we open every year
in the ground for her to swallow
the seeds that survived our
hunger and all the dead whole.
how do we not see the full picture,
but the two horns sticking
through the noose like the striking
aulos: a double reed. an angel lets
down the ram strapped to a parachute.
but this isn't the end of the tale
a ram is a lamb that didn't die
yet. the noose comes with its
mouth empty, the god missing.
you must look as the noose loosens
and the knife takes
its rightful place

## REBIRTH

*"i have my mother's mouth / and my father's eyes; on my face they are still together."*—warsan shire

       i was born upon the sign of the ram
       but i don't believe. i took my time to fuse

       onto your uterus & undid every webbed foot.
       the heart is always the first organ

       to form but i do not believe my heart
       when the tilapia we weaned from

       a flood backwater died in a bowl
       at the bottom of the stairwell.

## MILIARIA

on your upper right arm are spots
like a dark constellation. mother
calls them heat rash & this makes you feel
better, that you're not the cause
of your blemish & god's rejection
at the altar you carry like a millstone
around your neck. one day you will suffer
god to tell you what else you are
supposed to be if not *the ram*? one
day you will get a tattoo from that
lady at the dance hall to overwrite
the miliaria like blotches of a half-burnt offering.
you'll beg the snake to teach
you how to shed the miliaria
but it'll speak of the pain of losing
everything, the brief shame of nakedness
as you wait for new skin

# FATHER'S APOLOGY

you must know that i wouldn't turn a hungry knife in the flesh.
you must know that i had no say in all this. you must
know that i heard a wolf call & i couldn't resist for
it sounded so holy. you must know that the stars are spies
telling the sickle moon which way to face. you must know
that i prayed that the tinder wouldn't crack fire. you must know that
i tempted god thrice & wouldn't dare again.
you must know you're the harvest of a seed i was given &
i shall be faithful to the dust again. you must know that
i love my father with all his claws although i left.

do not be poisoned by your mother's delirium.
there's no antidote for the serpent at a crossroad.
i have not stopped grieving the moon's signal.
i am not cruel. only obedient. you must know that
the steel shrieks as it leaves its sheath. you must know that
i suffer my inner angel to hold my hand as i hold your neck.

## LIGHT-YEARS
*after caravaggio's* sacrifice of isaac

    in a past life, you're the still life painting
    the light took so long to enter. a constellation
    lies 290 light-years away from the earth.

    come, find the sky & all its dark matter. its
    sudden meteor shower like blood spurting
    from the ram's neck at the feast of the eid.

    drained, the man finds new color in the blood
    crust of communion wine. the platelets bind
    the bristles as the son bleeds from his eyes.

    for the half-light, you will have to tarry for
    days until the clot darkens a bit. for the shade
    between hemorrhage & blood meal. you lead

    the painter where he should go with his fingers.
    not by the pointillists' breadcrumbs. you lead
    the angel to the knife holding a hand in filicide.

    you hide every body part in canvas, so blessed
    is the man who can make a mouth & make it
    scream & stop at once. like centuries later,

    picasso's *weeping woman* & repin's *ivan*
    *the terrible*. like artemesia's *holofernes*
    like an ember holding its breath in a coal.

blessed is the mouth too for talking to a painter
in a language brief as the color covenant between
them. for heeding the sculptor's first creed:

a̋gbejű nı̋ı̋ b'amű ére jé̋. *beware, the chisel's
vanity as it carves & carves*. beware the bristles
stiffened like a cat's whiskers soaked in blood.

## ODE TO THE SERPENT

not the beast but the father
of tuba, son of a cornet
exiled from the cornet
family for lack of a thumb
hole. but the bronze
coiling staked in a hot
desert as the wind enters its
little windows into songs.
a breath reenters those
of us already smitten.
not the stealth of a silhouette
under curtain as it returned
again after repeated scare of
spell of the whisperer. but
its smoked remains, caged
in my aunt's *ayanran*
(among her amulets and pots
from jos) for the serpent never dies.
father, you're wrong, the snake
bothers us still. doesn't want to be
left alone. it wriggles through a wall
like an old song in my ear.
but years after that night, the mice took
the house, snipping uncle's chained tiger
generator wires with their incisors
filling the smoke chamber with fecal
matter until it gave the final cough
as we pulled its kick coiled inside
like a cobra. and that was the end

of light in the house. years after, saki
looked at the stars and said the aliens
would come for us. years later, we left.
she, too, left us. years later, the machine
coughed again with my auntie's final
breath of soot and poisoned lungs.

## POST-FLUVIAL MYTH WITH THE VEIL

the door is missing until i appear in a mist
of bath water. i was not mean once. come, be
unveiled again of my fleece like that time a boy
beheld his father naked in a mirage of hot shower
and spirits (and told no one until now; and this is
a secret we must keep to ourselves, promise me.
promise.) as he would one day see him again, for
final rites, as he washes the earth off the father's
body like every good son must, only to let him
down in the earth. the truth is he didn't mean to
look, but the door was missing. and the son must
lift the veil again. when he says, "you were not mean
once," he means me well, but will not be unkind to
the truth of it all. your paws stayed hidden
in woolen gloves when we were looking not for
wounds
but for the blood that binds us all. god wants
the child dead because there are enough to go round.
this is what we did not know until now. when the boy
lifts the veil, the father is robed in the fleece shorn
off the new sheep in the flock. in the festival of the
ram,
the boy thinks himself forsaken "you were not mean
once,"
the boy reminds me.

## MIRROR

*"ìyá ni wúrà; baba ni jígí*
the mother is gold; and father, mirror

        afraid of what i may discover, i blindfold
        every mirror at a night souk where a tooth
        fairy sells shiny things: obsidian & coins

        polished in a rain dream. i pawn away my
        canines for the saddest violin in stock. in
        the kitchen, a kettle howls over the flames

        as steam clouds the glass window. i wipe
        the fogged glass until i torture my face
        out of it. from a clear puddle in a coffin

        yard, the boxes could be a boat seen only
        briefly. & at once your eyes sweat an oasis
        of salt. lashes in a full lush. your irises bloom

        underwater. the *meruwa* wheels in a cart of water.
        he digs a well or a grave anywhere he goes.
        i buy my share of rain & behold, the water

        confesses all that's gnarled in me but not
        how to fix it. i immerse my shadow all day
        to catch the still fish of my reflection.

        i open my fish mouth but the waters never
        rush in. my words gurgle. in my language,
        we name our men after mirrors & mother-

of-pearls. i am the mica mired in clay. a false sheen. look at me, i churn every river after each catch. rippling a mirror's once steadfast face.

## GOOD FRIDAY

father is everything but a good snake
charmer. tell me, do you see only that
shiver in the hands and not the restless
animal steadied into a hole? in the fog
a wounded lamb limps. half of the sun
cobwebbed with clouds by cave spiders.
my tongue is a small sponge of vinegar.
and teeth, spittle-washed stalagmite. lip,
stone slab sealing the tomb endowed to
to the son in perpetuity. the lamb would
be unswallowed after three days & three
nights of indigestion. the tomb's gizzard
dulled— the cud bruised but alive! those
bite marks are visible from the cold nails.
like the lamb i want to herd my own
flock. but father shears his wool with his
own teeth and splits his hooves into claws.
the smoothness reveals a see-through wolf
throbbing beneath. father rubs honey for
ointment and palm oil for turning. the proverb
sets the wolf either free or on fire.
like me, the lamb is the father of the man.

## DEVOTION
*for george stinney jr., ellie mannette . . .*

i crouch under the safe dome of the sky. *ọba
k'òso, ọba k'òso.* a god hangs from a missing

rope. *the closest i ever came to god was in
a blur.* i feel so dizzy from believing. but any

river, scrubbed, holds no gospel, no flash of
a new fish & i long for the mud snake again.

i surrender to the arrow's one life. to the
steelpan, a bowl hollowed with many voices

as the *ajere*, the colander's wound, when stricken
by the pannist & i am stricken, lord. god! i bow

before the son seated on the electric chair—
long after his rushed crowning—a throne full

of power too much for him. the angels make way.
it's true that the crown crackled first with a *sẹkẹrẹ* rattle.

that the crackle grew to a lightning. we clap
knowing a song is heading toward silence.

## EPISTOLARY
*after yanni's "blue"*

dear chryssomallis, did you
have me in mind when you
sat by the grand piano as you
seanced alone through the dark
your paws scratching the ivory
keys. the wood is softest at the ivory
keys. the wood comes alive!
from the mutiny of flats & sharps
outnumbered by the white notes
& under these keybed slats are
ghouls holding the strings in place
alert & nervous like the spring
of a mouse trap, trapping the prey
released from your open paws into
its dark crevices.

o chryssomallis, summon me
by my name & i'll answer though

we're busy dying, holding our breath,
like that time at a beach where we toed
our names into the sand & watched the waves
claim them. later, we peeled off our buttons
& watched all false skin fall off. the sea drowns
so here goes my *alla a capella* to your growl.

o chryssomallis, the dead wood quickens
from within. there's a sphincter

somewhere in my voice. the dead aren't just sleeping,
they are dreaming of us

## NECROMANCY

it took my father thirty

years to catch up with his father's death.

ìyà n j'ẹsin, a'lọ́ m'ere sa.
*we name the horse's power after its long suffering.*

a foal loses its cart of go0ds, but we root for its
triumph, for loss, too, lightens a body.

ere t'ajá bán f'ogún odún sá ìrìn nif'ẹ́sin:
*a horse is a paw at rest.*

father daubs his napkin in tears
& starts. he says he's many bones missing
& a rib won't do. you can have many mothers
but only one god, many cowries but one revelation.

i am the boy who begs the fairy for more.

father wipes his father's portrait faster
until the frame squeaks, almost cracking
as if to breach the time-proof glass. he wipes the portrait
until his father's face brightens, clear as present,
but sad-eyed, as if grieving something beyond.

## ACKNOWLEDGMENTS

Thanks to thxe editors of the following journals where these poems have appeared usually under different titles and/or with further revisions:
*Grist:* "necromancy" (runner up for the ProForma contest)
*Guernica*: "good friday"
The line, *the closest I ever came to God was in a blur* in the poem "devotion" is borrowed from Nome Patrick's poem "The Body Walks through Grief towards God" in *Frontier Poetry*.